21st Century
Junior Library

LOVED ONES WITH CANCER

Loved Ones With

Lacey Hilliard and
AnneMarie McClain

Published in the United States of America by Cherry Lake Publishing Group
Ann Arbor, Michigan
www.cherrylakepublishing.com

Reading Adviser: Beth Walker Gambro, MS, Ed., Reading Consultant, Yorkville, IL
Book Designer: Jen Wahi

Photo Credits: cover: © JPC-PROD/Shutterstock; page 5: © fizkes/Shutterstock; page 6–7: © fototip/Shutterstock; page 8 (left): © ZOVICOTA/Shutterstock; page 8 (right): © goodbishop/Shutterstock; page 9: © IndianFaces/Shutterstock; page 10: © Thanakorn.P/Shutterstock; page 11 (top): © Lordn/Shutterstock; page 11 (bottom left): © NDAB Creativity/Shutterstock; page 11 (bottom right): © Tirachard Kumtanom/Shutterstock; page 12: © PorporLing/Shutterstock; page 13: © 1981 Rustic Studio kan/Shutterstock; page 14: © PintoArt/Shutterstock; page 16: © LightField Studios/Shutterstock; page 17: © SeventyFour/Shutterstock: page 18 (left): © Kaew LIVER/Shutterstock; page 18 (right): © WESTOCK PRODUCTIONS/Shutterstock; page 19: © The Creative Guy/Shutterstock; page 20–21: © Jose Luis Carrascosa/Shutterstock

Note from publisher: Websites change regularly, and their future contents are outside of our control. Supervise children when conducting any recommended online searches for extended learning opportunities.

Library of Congress Cataloging-in-Publication Data

Names: McClain, AnneMarie, author. | Hilliard, Lacey, author.
Title: Loved ones with cancer / written by AnneMarie McClain and Lacey Hilliard.
Description: Ann Arbor, Michigan : Cherry Lake Publishing, [2023] | Series: Loved ones with | Audience: Grades 2-3 | Summary: "Loved Ones With Cancer covers the basics of cancer, what people with cancer might experience, loving someone with cancer, and showing love for others and yourself. Loved Ones With explores what it's like to watch loved ones go through unique and often difficult circumstances. Written in kid-friendly language, this social-emotional learning series supports readers' empathetic understanding of these experiences not only for their loved ones, but also for themselves. Guided exploration of topics in 21st Century Junior Library's signature style help readers to Look, Think, Ask Questions, Make Guesses, and Create"– Provided by publisher.
Identifiers: LCCN 2023004589 | ISBN 9781668927335 (hardcover) | ISBN 9781668928387 (paperback) | ISBN 9781668928387 (ebook) | ISBN 9781668931332 (pdf)
Subjects: LCSH: Cancer–Patients–Family relationships–Juvenile literature. | Cancer–Juvenile literature.
Classification: LCC RC264 .M33 2023 | DDC 616.99/4–dc23/eng/20230214
LC record available at https://lccn.loc.gov/2023004589

Cherry Lake Publishing would like to acknowledge the work of the Partnership for 21st Century Learning, a network of Battelle for Kids. Please visit http://www.battelleforkids.org/networks/p21 for more information.

Printed in the United States of America
Corporate Graphics

CONTENTS

WHAT IS CANCER?

Cancer happens inside or on someone's body. Cells grow and divide in bodies. Cancer happens when cells that are not normal grow and spread.

Some types are skin cancer, lung cancer, leukemia, breast cancer, and prostate cancer.

Some cancers are harder to fight than others.

Different types of cancer can be more common than others. Some types are rare.

WHAT PEOPLE WITH CANCER MIGHT EXPERIENCE

Bodies may respond in different ways to cancer.

Cancer might affect how a person sleeps or eats. It might affect other activities. The person might not have much energy. Changes may happen slowly or quickly.

People with cancer may have many doctor's appointments.

Make a Guess!

What kinds of questions do you think scientists and care teams are asking about cancer?

Treatments may help people get better. People might try **chemotherapy** or **radiation therapy**. Other treatments or medicines may help.

There may be **medical procedures**. Some procedures involve removing a part of the body that has cancer or could get cancer.

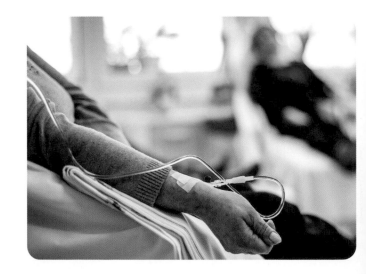

Cancer treatment looks different for each person with cancer.

Treatments might make people feel sick or tired. It may be hard to lift things. They may not be able to drive. They might feel fine on other days. Sometimes it is not possible to have treatments or procedures.

Some people might want to try treatments or procedures. Other people might not.

Some people may be open to treatment. Others may not be.

Sometimes families and friends want them to try things they don't want to try. Making decisions depends on many things. It depends on the person, their family, the care team, and the kind of cancer.

Each person's decisions about cancer treatment are unique.

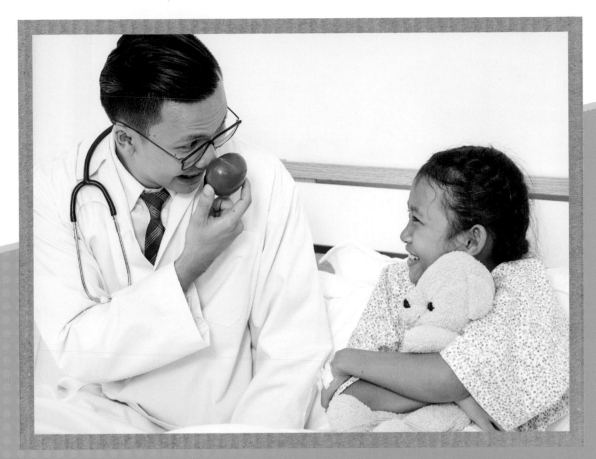

When people have cancer, they may feel disbelief, sadness, anger, fear, or worry. People may wonder what having cancer means. They may wonder how things could change. Sometimes people have hope they can get better.

Look!

This kid's body is working hard to fight cancer. Their care team and family help them.

It is okay to feel all kinds of emotions when someone you love has cancer.

14

LOVING SOMEOME WITH CANCER

If someone you love has cancer, you might feel all kinds of emotions. You might not know how to feel. You might feel like cancer came out of nowhere. You might wish you could make it go away. It is okay to feel however you feel. It can be hard to see someone have cancer.

Think!

How could you be a friend to someone who has cancer? How could you be a friend to someone whose loved one has cancer?

You might notice changes to their body. Changes can be losing hair. Changes can be using a wheelchair. They are still the person you love.

You might visit your loved one at the hospital. There you may see wires and machines with beeping noises. You may notice different smells. Tubes or bandages may be on your loved one. Doctors and nurses may come in and out of the room.

You might go to the hospital to visit your loved one. You may come across things you haven't seen before.

In the hospital, your loved one may have some tubes attached to them. There may be machines making noises. These are things to help your loved one.

17

SHOWING LOVE FOR OTHERS AND YOURSELF

There are things you can do to show love for them and for yourself.

You might want to create more memories together. You might want to think about your favorite times together. You might want to look at pictures or take new ones.

You can focus on helping yourself feel better. You might want to show your loved one how much they mean to you. You can enjoy things you like doing.

If a family member has cancer, grown-ups around you might need to focus a lot of attention on them. You can ask for time with your grown-ups. People in the same family can need different things.

Things to know:

Cancer is not contagious. You can spend time with your loved one and not worry about getting sick.

Create!

Create a plan for what you could do to help people with cancer in your community. What are some ways to show love?

Ask Questions!

Scientists and care teams are learning to help people fight cancer. Ask a grown-up to help you learn more. What good news can you find?

There are many people who survive and recover from many kinds of cancer. Sometimes cancer can make people die. It is not fair how that works.

Sometimes even after people survive cancer, they act, move, speak, or look different. They are still themselves.

Scientists and doctors are working to understand cancer. They want to stop cancer and help people. Helpers make things better for people with cancer and their loved ones.

21

GLOSSARY

breast cancer (BREHST KAN-ser) cancer of breast tissue cells; breast tissue cells are part of your chest

cells (SEHLZ) the smallest living part of organisms; some cells are organisms themselves

chemotherapy (kee-moh-THAIR-uh-pee) using medicine to kill cancerous cells

contagious (kuhn-TAY-juhs) able to be spread and caught by others

disbelief (dihs-buh-LEEF) when someone has trouble believing what is happening or what they have been told

emotions (ih-MOH-shuhnz) feelings

Leukemia (loo-KEE-mee-uh) cancer of white blood cells; white blood cells fight infections and other diseases

lung cancer (LUHNG KAN-ser) cancer of lung cells; lung cells make up the lungs

medical procedures (MEH-dih-kuhl proh-SEE-jurz) something a medical expert does to help someone or to see what is going on

prostate cancer (PRAH-stayt KAN-ser) cancer of prostate cells; prostate cells make up the prostate organ

radiation therapy (ray-dee-AY-shuhn THAIR-uh-pee) using radiation to kill cancerous cells

recover (ruh-KUH-ver) to get better

skin cancer (SKIHN KAN-ser) cancer of skin cells

LEARN MORE

Books:

Hair for Mama by Kelly A. Tinkham; Dial Books for Young Readers

The Lemonade Club by Patricia Polacco; Philomel Books

You Are the Best Medicine by Julie Aigner Clark; Balzer + Bray

Search online for the following video resources with an adult:

HiHo Kids – "Kids Meet a Kid with Cancer"

Leukemia & Lymphoma Society – "Kids Just Like You - What Is Cancer?"

INDEX

ABOUT THE AUTHORS

Lacey Hilliard is a college professor, researcher, and parent. Her work is in understanding how grown-ups talk to children about the world around them. She particularly likes hearing what kids have to say about things.

AnneMarie McClain is an educator, researcher, and parent. Her work is about how kids and families can feel good about who they are. She especially loves finding ways to help kids and families feel seen in TV and books.